EACH BLOSSOM MAKES HORSES TREMBLE

EACH BLOSSOM MAKES HORSES TREMBLE

Glen Downie

Mansfield Press

Printed in Canada

Library and Archives Canada Cataloguing in Publication

Title: Each blossom makes horses tremble / Glen Downie.
Names: Downie, Glen, author.
Description: Poems.
Identifiers: Canadiana 2020037205X | ISBN 9781771262521 (softcover)
Classification: LCC PS8557.O84 E23 2020 | DDC C811/.54—dc23

Cover Photo: D. Hall
Typesetting & Cover Design: Denis De Klerck

The publication of *Each Blossom Makes Horses Tremble* has been generously supported by the Canada Council for the Arts and the Ontario Arts Council.

ONTARIO ARTS COUNCIL
CONSEIL DES ARTS DE L'ONTARIO
an Ontario government agency
un organisme du gouvernement de l'Ontario

Canada Council for the Arts
Conseil des arts du Canada

Mansfield Press Inc.
25 Mansfield Avenue, Toronto, Ontario, Canada M6J 2A9
Publisher: Denis De Klerck
www.mansfieldpress.net

... some words remain forever fallen.
And sometimes we find such words
...
as if they knew someone was going to come
gather them up and build a new language,
a language made up entirely of fallen words.

– Roberto Juarroz

NORMAL SASKATCHEWAN

Always in a foreign country the poet uses poetry
as an interpreter.

– Edmund Jabès

Cleanliness helps us make
the most of ourselves

*

The telephone system is to keep us warm

*

Two boys were poor brothers
and sisters
It was too much trouble to do this
But he did not think that
looks were important

*

The first job shone   He never even
thought of a torn place

*

Do you know whether the skin you see
is your true skin?

*

Things you buy in the store
are alive

You have windows in the skin
Pull a curtain over your windows

*

Hairs grow if the glass is strong
Inside is the true language

*

You cannot see rain-drops standing in the road
You may
– floating –
after a boat has passed

*

Nerves make it possible for you
to learn things

Pain flows in a circle from the heart

*

Have you noticed how red the room is?
One of the reasons you wear clothes

*

The lost water has gone

People who contain tiny holes poured out
the many rivers of Canada

*

Sleep out of doors in dark
blood   Have you noticed girls
have a jolly look?
When they can no longer get food
they are changed

*

In some schools girls
file their fingernails
so the rest may learn
Brothers and sisters often help
slicing finger tips   It does not
hurt   The surface is not alive

*

Lean over small insects

*

Wear only your hat
This is what boys and girls learn:
orangewood

*

Ask a grown person to rub a little olive oil
until they feel comfortable
It is very hard
to break the habit

Remember how you feel when
you get a new hat

You feel happy

*

In business
your chances of success are better
if you do not have to be ashamed

*

Sore collection of necks
irritates his helper   The caterpillar
would have seemed pleasanter
if he had not been smoking

*

Columbus had hollow limbs   Indians
breathed smoke all over the world
Noses were cut off

People have argued there is no death
may be too much

Sometimes a doctor is a difference of opinion

*

Canada wants her children
Do your part

*

Are you doing your best to be good-looking?
When you start for school in the morning
do you ask yourself

Are my hands hollows?
Do you sleep every night out of doors?

*

Choose the best book   The book should be washed
every month   Missing words

write the book The skin is protected from harm by
little pits The only way skin can be cleaned is by
wearing your hat Have you ever thought of yourself
as a walking advertisement? How many advertisements
are on your list? If possible look at your skin
Make a drawing of what you see

*

Have you ever heard anyone say this or that?
Find out what the person meant

*

Have a manicure Ask children to come and watch
Give attention to each thing in the list
How often must you do it?

*

Find out something For example
why the fine silver?
What do you know about air?
the meaning of *normal*?

*

Select which things appear
larger than they really are
Nails flow in a circle
the way a person looks

*

What has laughter to do with how to be hungry?

Sometimes the way you feel
interferes with a person   He may become
anxious   The roof
smelled like a joke she heard at school
Can you think of one?

*

Think of ways you can make people
smile in the Middle Ages

*

You usually eat cake in every period
of history   Chewing
is quickly learned   Pleasant thoughts
as you eat
all the water you like

*

Water cannot change
Only juices do that

There is no food in the mouth based on
good taste   Hands are less likely
to make boiling water   They

may have picked up soup
noiselessly   making
as little clatter as possible

*

Drop crumbs on the floor   forgetting
to say thank you   It takes an hour

by slow degrees   Think of
working the radio   Take apart the materials:
bones teeth hair muscle and blood

*

Make false hair   false teeth
with great trouble and expense   The workshop
must be twenty-five feet long   It looks thin
taken apart   If you mix sand

sugar will not dissolve   These materials are found
in the coarse outer parts of Canada

*

Real hair is folded in space
below the building

If the work is slowed up   You feel
tired and cross
your skin may look muddy

*

Food is about five feet long

*

The work you do not have
makes the body suffer
Always obey desire
Blood is left over
even if you use every scrap

*

This must be sent out or you will die
You cannot see when your mother turns
to carbon   Each time you breathe   the work
done by the body lies on each side   A small
bag holds the most important thing
you can do

*

The best time to eat sweets
is before they have a chance

*

Are you cheerful?
Do you do what you can?
Do you wash the table hard for half an hour?
Do you brush your teeth every six months?

*

Reword each false statement
to make it true

The book passes into the stream
hindered by worry
anger or tiredness

You can train ice-water to play in your home

*

What would happen if
the ashes were taken?

Use this experiment to explain

the lump of sugar

Ask the butcher to fill
the skin with sugar

Taste the water   How
does it taste?   Plan amusements

*

Only three generations have known one
all their lives

Do you know a Greek boy?

*

You talk about goodness and beauty –
is there a map that shows this country?

Look closely
Not many are born perfect

They thought that minds could be trained
to love the true
seek knowledge
show courage
be gentle and kind

Is this not what we mean?

*

A curved paper-cutter was supposed to give
happy thoughts   fit for society

Do you know any girls
popular at parties?

*

A boy learned
with a sharp-pointed stick
to write long poems

History grew your book
like a long boot

*

There was a time when people
were masters of all they knew

Place a compass on the toe
and you will have an idea

*

The greatest bathers the world has ever known
rich and poor alike
many miles away ...

Do you live in a city?

The air sweet with perfume   Coloured stones
decorated the mind   A scraper made of bone
with a silver handle

*

Hundreds of years went by   People lived in little huts
Unheard of – the rich picking up

germs on their sticky feet   Children played
in the mud   water hanging in the fireplace   Wood-ashes
and grease so strong it hurt the skin

*

How surprised those girls would be! Rain-water
caught washing dishes! Kings and queens now known
and fully appreciated

*

People used to think it was dangerous
to learn about beautiful things

Your mother would have given you
a rag soaked in vinegar

*

A wise man discovered France is
a very old country

How long should you have to think back?

There are tiny forms of life
which cause death

*

We cannot see by looking

Do you like bread?
Think of all you carried to your door-step
Take great price in shining

*

No one knows what cold looks like
No one has ever seen it

Cold makes us uncomfortable
even the shepherd was fooled

Night shut up the shepherd
and killed him on the spot

*

Bed is the place for a person who may not go
Delay in going to bed a danger to everyone

*

No medicine can cure the newspapers
A person becomes the slave of the drug
– a foolish risk

If they call him   he may leave cold spoons
on a good citizen

Do not leave them lying about for someone else to pick up

*

Some people get smaller   A person
who has two or three drinks
loses more

*

Coal smoke cannot

put up a good fight
Is it foolish to form habits?

Do you know what happens when you are not there?

Does the room look the same in the morning?
Fresh paper! When the girls come back
they are welcomed by clean shining pencils
telling about things they should do

*

Are you doing your best to keep the ground muddy?
Do you put fruit in your hat?
Do you put your belongings
in the proper cups and glasses?

*

Do not write *anoint*
wood-ashes
good citizen

A great teacher lived in a body many miles distant

Soap discovered true and false

A good rule is never a common cup

*

Are you expected to be clean?
Is it harder for an unclean person to get ahead?
Find out what you can about
how they keep their bodies   Ask
your parents or grandparents   Form committees

*

Water is brought into town   Find out where
What is done to keep the water pure?
Your teacher may visit the place   If
you like to write stories
write a story   Explain
the difference between taking a bath
in Canada today and long ago

*

The source of life is moist
moving
rosy

Do you know what special arrangements
the nose has?

Do you know the principal differences between
jelly fish and a baby?

Perfect food is colourless
You are breathing it now

Scientists are sure that no beasts live on the moon

a huge ball of rock which does not know
the wonder of life

*

Of course it is possible
to breathe through your mouth
Open your mouth now
and see the dust

*

By taking a narrow path   winding
over hills and down valleys   there is more
time for things to happen

Usually the bleeding will stop

Do not wash away the blood

*

The branches of a tree become smaller and smaller
until finally they end
in wintertime

Have you ever *seen* when cold
strikes
with every breath?

You cannot see the results of two things that happen

*

Doors in motion
feel more alive   Your brain
can work better in fresh moving air

Wind spoke the Latin language

Speaking of a breeze
experiments have been made

These experiments feel sleepy
lose interest   Great care is now taken
to hang in a place

where you can read easily

*

Ordinary is dry and dusty
colder than the body
In cities   smoke pours
from delicate diseases

Make room for old used air
in churches   factories   trains

Sometimes a person feels faint
Always lean toward the sun

*

Tissues have power

The flesh: how sad
we should be without it

Shut up prisoners
cut holes in the sun

*

The bone building   usually placed near
the body ...

Fall directly on bare skin   Do not go
through glass while playing

There are not many ordinary foods
The richest doctors give their children
bones   Rays

shine on the milk from special
cows   Children in wintertime
are soft and crumbly

*

Give yourself to the morning   Shade the sun
for fifteen minutes
with your face rooted in one spot

*

A jelly-fish as he grows older
begins writing
skating
jumping rope
playing games

There is a right way of holding
body organs: crowded closely together

Stand
sit
and walk in a graceful manner

Take this position without thinking:
sway forward   stiffen
your knees   forget

Hold your head high
as a fifteen-storey building
made of beautiful white stone

*

Twenty-six bones

held together with jars ...

Do not make trouble
People become flat very quickly

*

There is a law: the body must shrink
and wither

Can you remember the first time
you ever did anything?

Your brain felt worn out when school was over
The fuel runs low

*

You can train your mind to use sunshine

His legs did not belong to him   troubles
make them fly away

*

Do you read out of doors every pleasant day?
Are you trying to show good form?
Supply the missing word

*

The best people –
wearing ordinary clothes   eating
only bread and water –
need more sleep

Do you like the way you look?
How do your mouth and throat feel?

Good posture might
help a person give reasons

*

Walter is unhappy whether
he wins or loses   Marion

lonesome

goes off by herself and cries

*

Show your skill and bravery by
saving someone's life
Watch for small beginnings
when someone's clothing
catches fire

*

People come home from war without a scratch
to slip in the bathtub and break a rib:
a good occupation for a rainy day

Headquarters will provide this for a small charge

*

Stand on a rocking chair to straighten a picture
Nail the matchbox high up where Don can't reach it
Stick pins will remind people that contain poison

to keep a light burning in the pots on the stove

*

Practice tends to soften and thaw
surfaces thus darkened

Treacherous five-year-old twins nodded solemnly

*

A spark has no place   The greatest damage
occurs when the fires are out
in the spring of the year

Signs are whiteness   numbness
Place a frozen hand under an arm
Call loudly for help by tying clothes together
Weigh one end with a person in trouble   Be careful
not to let him grab you

*

It is not fun to be poisoned
The people who have the most fun
learn beforehand to
keep things from happening

Good holes will have blunt scissors
and a small bottle   Leave the cut place
to keep from becoming infected
Dangerous ones are bruised
and torn at the edges

*

Are you doing the best things?
Are you helping to build bonfires?
Do you paint children's toys with frost-bite?
Do you know a drowning person?

*

We are safe as long as we are broken:
annoying
but not really dangerous

A rocking chair the principal cause
of the kitchen fire

Frost-bite is an older person
– some may spoil your vacation –
issued by the Department of Pensions

*

Your family cannot send you where you would like

Think about who was the real hero

Little Rose began to scream   Ned pulled Rose to the floor
Was Ned's action wise?

Make a map of your home and all the danger

*

Be sure you can pronounce
friction
acid
rusting

Write a sentence telling what you think
when you see each one

*

So many garments are made
in great factories   Boys and girls everywhere
wear the same clothes   Do you know why
rubber coats should be taken off?   Do you know
a sparrow may have good-looking shoes?

*

We find human beings with thin skins
in every corner   Do you have pictures?

Warmth is in you   One way of catching fish
is to hold cloth up to the light

*

Wind is just another name
for the body   Have you ever seen

a sparrow?   It is
full of tiny holes   Little holes
catch air

*

We do not know sheep but we do know
very old women who lived in Europe
All the rooms were cold   They learned to make
glass and paper   They invented a kind of writing
and divided time into
years that people from other countries

still go to see

*

People wove grasses into garments   No one knows
how long it took them –
twenty-five hundred years?
Many people earned their living
moving air through little holes   White people
go to the tropics about eighteen times a minute

*

A room open top and bottom
does not easily take up moisture
Underwear gets very cold in the light
By wearing galoshes Queen Elizabeth
ruled over England   Their heads were
carried on platters so big that
ladies could not pass each other on narrow streets

*

In the nineteenth century   women
could hardly breathe   Girls
would grow small   Boys were not obliged

*

In the country
in the mirror
in the little room next to Edna's
your bones grow out of shape
Little wonder!

Toes became so long

they had to be tied to the knees
so the person could walk

Nowadays more attention is given the feet

*

Harm may be done longer
on a clean sheet of paper

X-ray machines show the bones of the salesman
He may feel comfortable when you are sitting
but when you stand up
the pain will go shining in the spaces between

*

In order to keep sweet-smelling   boys your age
should be washed in clear water   If possible
hang them outdoors to dry

*

Many boys and girls brighten their morning with
a special hook

*

Do you change your underwear twice a week?
Keep your shoes shined? Hang up your hat?
Do not write the book
made of hard dead skin

*

What does this tell you about people

if you find a library in your attic?   Can you
think of any reason clothes are better-looking?
Make an outline of North America and the feet
along the street   Draw pictures
Make a play   Demonstrate
the washing of stockings

*

Name a committee to make a simple coat hanger
Be sure you know the meaning of *miserable*

*

Make sentences using blanks   Exchange your sentence
with those of another   Labour is work   Scientists have
the right or wrong ideas about things

*

They are brothers   Why is the other so thin?
The brown coats had been removed   What is the matter?
The other child's legs bend out like bows every pleasant day

*

Bones keep growing for years   Food
is a board full of nails   You can understand this
by breathing on a mirror

*

Small material is left which will not burn: ash

Less than one grain of salt   yet if that grain is lacking
all sailors disappear from English ships

*

American scientists working on the mystery
had no family name   We call each one
by a letter of the alphabet

*

Joan   a good-looking intelligent girl   had
peculiar eating habits: hot dry fruit
in pretty glasses
or stewed prunes

Joan's brothers eat their cups and plates

Last year Joan drank
only cocoa   She thought it a bother
to eat a whole orange

Joan became cross   Everyone else
became white rats

*

The longest meals need vitamin D

*

All you get for your money is pleasant flavour
How many fountains are in *your* neighbourhood?
Living disease may be carried from the lips   A man
beats a horse; a horse is apt to be nervous

*

Many grown-ups find pleasure in drinking

These drinks speed up the heart   whip
their bodies   They like it because
they are used to it

*

Girls would rather drink whale oil
than chocolate soda

*

People in the South Sea Islands would rather
blubber than obey signals   How ridiculous!
One drop of energy lost
in a bucket of harm!

*

In every country of the world   no one feels much
like eating   Even death is a good answer   Write
the book   Choose the best ending

*

When the life records of drinkers are compared
with those of a school cafeteria
which are wise? Which are foolish?

Have all your salad except the lettuce
        mustard on cheese with pickles instead of tea
        white bread liver candy soda and frankfurters

Do you ever refuse to burn cabbage leaves?

*

You can learn to like dentists   Keep them
in bottled sunshine   Carry on an experiment

White rats turn blue in a fireproof dish using
the menus on page 164   Do not write the book
in a very old language

*

Perfect eyes cannot see
the mountains of the moon
yet the mountains *are* there   One day
he peered at clear rain-water and saw
swarming animals   That was a great day!

*

Two hundred years went by   He could not know
how great it was   He lived a busy
happy life   He was ninety-one
when he fell into the hands
of children working in the dark

*

A Dutch boy no one had ever seen
made careful drawings:
things too small   weak
and strong   the scarlet dark

*

As far back as you can remember you have been told
to keep away from people   Kings would have given
a fortune for the knowledge any boy has today

Your great-grandparents knew nothing better
than to run away

Poor parents! The road led to
the souring of milk

*

Other scientists said “No! How can you say that?”
The battle between scientists went on furiously
and lo!   it belongs to a family
of tiny living things   Thick cloudy material is called
the mother

Leaves lying on damp ground start to rot   Leaves
may not be harmful but they are certainly annoying

*

Friendly plants make a special kind
of living   From the earliest periods of history
your mother probably throws away a can of peaches
Poison dulls the mind   makes a person do
queer things   It is a great shame

*

Some boyhood friends found
a way he could kill them   Many people died
though a doctor did his best

a kind-faced doctor

It made him very sad

*

A friend advised him to read about sewers   He
washed his hands

He is the father   He worked all his life
with a hot iron until
slightly scorched   Great heat destroys

*

Your home may not be pure   Few people get it
Never pick food that bites

*

Have you seen a door which says *Scarlet*?
Your board of health is trying to protect boys
in your community   It is good never to go
even when there is no sign   You cannot be sure that
the illness is not catching   You will have the satisfaction
of knowing you are a good soldier

*

Try to stay cheerful about staying by yourself
Make it a rule not to kiss anyone
                    allow yourself to be kissed
                    go to parties
                    or travel

having fun
in your own yard

*

He dreamed that the forest melted away   In its place
stood little houses built inside out   The young man

stood in darkness although the sun was shining
His spirit will always have the power
to kill in large numbers

*

Sick houses are getting well   Tears
with which your eyes are always bathed
make an antidote

*

Almost everybody had
the terrible disease   The ones who did not die
were left with scars – the whole body was covered

Chicken-gristle soup had become
stale and weak   He decided to use it anyway
They did not die   They remained
living in a cow

*

The blood of horses killed over months
is far better than rats
mice and flies

*

Are you deeper than a scratch?
Are you careful never to sneeze?
Do you help your mother throw away
all food   careful
never to eat anything?

*

Do not write Louis   Edward
Joseph   Anton   Every
communicable disease
is caused by a special kind of living

*

What are the names of harmful plants with eyes?
Why is the fight so difficult?
A plant likes water and sunlight   How may you make
conditions inside your body favourable?

*

Do these things: wash a white potato
thoroughly
wash it again about 45 minutes

Examine the potato every day
At the end of a week fill two small glasses
half full of fresh sweet milk   Put one glass
in a warm dark place   put the other in some

cold dark place   At the end of four days
get two perfect apples   With a blunt dirty knife
cut through your skin   When you cut through your skin
ask a committee

which members have communicable diseases
Make a chart to show what committee protects a person
from getting the disease

*

Tim was kicking time
in his sleep   While you are growing

you need people
whose growing time is over

*

You grow in your sleep   Some employers
allow their employees a few minutes
at certain times during the day

Do you know what it means to people?
Dangerous rest during leisure time?

*

The mending must be put off
Your heart pumps less   Muscles work
only when you change

Your brain never gets rest   A door may slam
far off in the distance   Your brain tells you
who slammed the door   Voices
sound far away   Pictures in your mind
become shadowy   At last
you have lost your senses

*

They pile up in the blood   The delicate body
has a chance to free itself   If dogs are kept awake
they die   People sleep standing up   Children
blame their mothers   It is best
to take the word
of the scientists   What does a train do?

*

Light in your eyes   Your brain kept busy
answering trouble calls   You have
dreams   The chief enemies
are milk wagons   People are requested
not to talk or laugh   Older people
taking afternoon naps when you come home
walk on tiptoe

The shades might shut out
refreshing breezes   Any boy or girl who is handy
can tie dark material over the eyes   Strips
of tissue move in a slight
breeze   A board may be used
or a blanket hung over two chairs

*

They thought night air gave them fever   We know now
two Italian words
will keep mosquitoes out   You cannot sleep
if you are cold or warm or loaded

What position do you usually take? Do you change
this position? No one sees you in bed

Do not think about your looks   That makes
the heart beat faster   Perhaps it is impossible
for you to sleep alone now
Some day when you begin to earn money ...

*

One boy trained himself to arrange his mind
before getting up   Which kind
of boy or girl are you?   It is pleasant
the day you leave the house   Some people

do not even notice the sun is shining   Take time out now
to let your muscles go limp   Look off into the distance
The day is over

*

One popular hobby is collecting stamps
flowers
butterflies
coins
shells
pebbles
dolls
china
models
music
books

Leisure is your time to do as you please
one little corner in life where you are different

*

Do you have thoughts that disturb the sleep of others?
Are you very much interested in something? Give a reason
for wearing underwear
having a large fat pillow
playing exciting games before bed-time

*

Think why it is harder to get
evening amusements   Must you give up
the pictures?   Keep an eleven-year-old
plan of sleep   Test air movements
by tying tissue to furniture   Think

of ways you may overcome

Plan meals choosing milk
soup
creamed vegetables
soft-boiled eggs
stewed fruits
custard
gelatine
Be sure you know the meaning of *malaria*
affair ...

Make sentences with words missing   Exchange
your sentences with another pupil
Try to complete the sentences she has made

*

People who depend on magic
wish to get something for nothing   Do you know
what signals to make
when you ask a stranger for a ride?

*

Some thoughtless car-drivers are wicked enough
after alcohol

*

Boys and girls who own bicycles should
take proper care – good practice for when you have
an airplane   Stealing a ride on the back is not fair   Besides

jumping off a boy may be
run over

*

Why must everyone stop talking? Every three minutes
a child is injured   every two hours a child is killed   Never
give a child handlebars   Do not ask a stranger to give you
his automobile   Do you like to be interrupted?

*

Sometimes a child will dart into the street
to blame the truck-driver who could not
stop in time   One side-walk game is Watch Your Step
Another is drawn in the shape of a snail

*

Water   like fire   is a friend
that may turn into an enemy
Do not change places with anyone

*

You should read this book walled-in
in all directions by bone   But
a sharp-pointed instrument
directly enters the eye   You can learn more
about the eye by looking at it than you can learn
about the ear by hearing it – the little hallway
leading from the outside world

*

The odour of wax is disagreeable   Never try to
remove an insect with giant firecrackers
In everyday life people do not wear helmets   They trust
each other not to do things

*

You enjoyed testing eyesight   Test your hearing also
Place a watch against your ear

Move away

*

Do not write the book when riding in traffic
In walking a country highway   show the policemen
the deaths and injuries to people on foot last year
Include twenty-five cents to pay the cost of steering gear
Write a sentence telling what you think of
good citizen   police department

WILDLY SUCCESSFUL

Look at the flower and the flower also looks

– Zen koan

If you think *unwanted*
unattractive

open your eyes!
Suckle morning!

Learn blackberry bramble

a tall field
close-up

*

Tricky corn crops
in a soybean field
do not have status

They have been east
making civilization possible

*

Primitive farmers
rearing their pretty heads
where others
wish they would not

are quite beautiful   Makes sense
to get to know them
serve coffee
dandelion wine

*

Several shades
of meaning:

how stout is stout anyway?

*

Unnecessary terms
weeded out

Be on the lookout for a picture
worth a thousand words

*

Ancient farmers
lost to us
applied blue dye to the English
making the landscape attractive

*

Defined by unwantedness
the mere mention of its name
will bring blood to the whites of the eyes

The strawberry one man's enemy
another's good friend

*

You need to know
there are no peasants

Definitions depend on
the one defining

Attributes:

their rank
wild growth

their aggressive habits

their persistence
resistance to control

their ability
to see evil

*

Pioneers of succession
condemned without fair trial

A lazy farmer cannot be expected

It was Man who opened up
the happiest spots

Man tore his clothes
Animals scattered them
across the continent

*

Fires
floods
other disturbances
have occurred

but lawns are not natural   Man
the chief disrupter of relationships

*

Friends in the frightening New World
made their escape over fence and wall

*

Butter and eggs came unbidden
unsuspected

attached to clothes
or fur

The foreign from Europe
credit
their pioneering ability

*

On a hot August afternoon
when leaves are hanging down
like the ears of a beagle

the cultivated can be heard to pant

*

Weedy species have grown
a greater number of hairs
Their vigour is obvious

This is the large tribe

*

The eye sees a single flower
spiral toward the centre
with its private parachute

Passing human beings
are carried great distances
before being brushed away

*

When you point to a tree and say "Bark!"
you are not entirely correct
in Brooklyn

A five-thousand-year-old pine
does not die

*

The dead

– tiny clearer areas
of varying shapes –

permit the exchange
so necessary
to life

*

Where ferns grow
as erect tall trees

note the eyes:

all that is left of the normal

*

Crocus is overlapping food

Swollen leaves are small editions

Inflorescence:
poetry

*

Scientists define everything

I prefer the poet
– so few lovely words –
prostrate on the ground:

Repent!
Repent!

A very special nuisance

*

Fox
grape
leaflets
wild cucumber:

each alone
and different from all others

*

If two face each other
there are three

*

Our blanket
upon which all life depends:

grass
and nothing more!

*

If tomorrow were to fail
you and I would be doomed

Everything loves the waters of our planet

The time has come to give
more thought to this

*

Leaf falls at the approach
of winter:
more easy to see

*

When they are hidden by leaves
the gardeners of Japan
learn what really is occurring

Branch out to each other!
Radiate!

*

Like fingers on a hand
the common household

Keep in mind
horizontal sisters
all attached

You have created a giant

*

Always felt sorry for roots

one main
conspicuous
dominating root

Select a fresh carrot
Study it closely

Small thin branches come
from wrinkles

The carrot of commerce
not your own

Leave a small piece
way down deep

*

Ancient peoples carried
the male to the female

A religious ceremony
rewards the visiting animal

*

The word gives the story away:
wind-loving

Do not put on a big show
Grasses are wind

*

When grain grows out of grain
the stigma ...

The chamber where the egg awaits
has been accomplished

Interesting that
the huge watermelon
is a ripened ovary

*

There are two possibilities:
it may open
or it may not

Suture
black locust
evening:

not all open

The strawberry is by no means a berry

Open it with a razor
You will see

*

Grass family:
the point of attachment
not visible

You can make this structure out
with a sharp razor blade

Look inside
You can see the future

*

Remove this skin
So tough it is almost impossible

Join each other perfectly
like a little feather

No need to call

Shrivel up
and fall away

*

Their upper surfaces
closely together

their lower surfaces pressed against
the act

until the last moment
then unfolding
and turning in the light

*

Why include a tree?
Few trees attain maturity

Birds drop
from telephone wires
neither attractive
nor valuable
in this condition:

reddish brown
bright green
shiny on their upper surfaces
with small incurving teeth

White flowers appear in May   Later
fruits black and bitter
the most dangerous wild cherries:
ten times the cyanide

*

Stones
west to the Dakotas

give rise
to new plants

*

Some orphans were playing and fell
into a stupor

seventy-five feet high
very fragrant   with wings

*

Tree of heaven survives
under adverse conditions:
tenement walls
garbage-filled lots

Large
horseshoe-shaped scars
give off a vile odor
The wind carries it

*

Composed: three leaflets
delicious as food

*

Climbing is lovely

Once escaped
it will cover large areas
with its spreading
everything

*

Wild morning
more valuable glory

bell-shaped
heart-shaped
hiding

The field
one inch across at best

*

Flowers are exactly opposite
The fruit is a grape but a berry

*

Few are more disliked
or feared

The vine is often confused

Midwinter is dangerous to Man
though animals seem safe

Birds eat without ill effects

Taking a bath in crushed leaves
is excellent protection

*

Blue cow titters

The lovely one-sided rain
tips desirable plants under it

each of which ends
in a soft olive green

sensitive to salt

*

Blue inflorescence: the tendril
end of the leaf

the power denoted by X

*

Virginia: disturbed
by most definitions

Poor Virginia has been burned
hacked
uprooted

Sporting
not selective of companions

may be found climbing the same
quite sensitive wall

*

As children   we punks
let them burn slowly
savouring their odor

We were smoking cigars   Are there
such innocents anymore?

*

Hollow in between

away from its higher
or lower neighbour

found on poorly drained ground
surrounded by three smooth leaves

*

Brings tears to the eyes
the slender
underground winter
tipped by a tail

head the size of a wheat grain

Bread made from these
will be unmarketable

*

Poverty rush
wire grass ...

Walk down early some morning
Your shoes are the seeds
of the path Man makes
through fields

Someone not trained is
not harsh and strawlike –
they are real

This slender rush seems happy

*

Timothy has escaped
and become a cotton sound
in the mountains
Terminal
recognizable
dies next year

Value
increases as the season
advances

*

Foxtail
a poor man's cereal
looks like a bottle brush

May be dangerous
producing disturbances

*

Cool moist summers are ideal
high and smooth
pressed closely against
a concave space

One of the authors of the Bible
Aristotle
knew this

*

MAN THREE FEET TALL
FOUND ON LITTLE BLUE STEM!

A fertile one
Filmy hairs give bearded appearance –
wolf
poverty
wild states

*

Touch the ground:
a blessing to the farmer

Strawberry: let it
fill the spaces

Scatter straw
shorter finger-grass from the hand
bright red blood between
midspring
summer
first frost

*

Often confused
thick
flat
weak

used in poor sections of Europe
in which a temple was found

*

Panic reproduces
clandestinely
its nature not announced

One may wonder ... What is the agent?
Wind?

*

Few people survive for nine years
in the soil: troublesome thought

Famine-pale ribs
spreading panic
in rice
and carrot fields

*

Redtop
purpletop
Florida and Texas

Old fields
open woods
waste grounds
and gardens

Striking
the first
students are impressed

When the time comes to squeeze
you feel this
stickiness

*

Chess cheat: widespread
in the Southeast
Waste places beautiful
at maturity   Purple plumes

nod in the wind

*

It is hard to imagine anyone in our country

gathered for their aesthetic qualities

Nodding heads can be
boiled and eaten like a potato

*

Day escapes from gardens
lasts but a day

While beautiful
it tends to run wild

*

Widow's tears of the eighteenth century
tell you: the brothers
have been killed

The third died
before accomplishing anything

*

The day is attractive but
may not have a chance

From Asia   the spider
has bright blue
smaller
neglected fields

*

Do not make the erroneous assumption
that this crown sits on a relative

Spikes like pins
in a cushion introduced from Europe
range throughout waste places

*

The common white man
grows on the highroads
in great quantities

Indians never grew here

Wherever a European walked
this grew in his footsteps

*

Greater dooryard
unattended
safe from depredations

Weedy species put to use by Man

Seeds of the closely related
overcome sluggishness

In antient writers
three roots will cure one griefe

*

It is possible to bake
palatable bread
during politically stressful moments

Napoleon has been found

in long dead
completely preserved
human stomachs

*

The troublesome valley reminds me
of early grammar school
We were unaware

and sweet little girls
clung with just
the right tenacity
for our evil purposes

*

Bitter Nova Scotia sister
the New York City subways
are guiltless

When all its requirements are met
watchfulness and attention
should help you catch
any rough-hairy male

*

The common causes
– so much human suffering –
stammer south to Texas

*

Vulgaris
Nothing chaste about

Oscar Wilde
famous relative and felon

actively fond of the moon
vacant lots and
absinthe   a drink
dangerous to consume

*

Repeat this incantation
while rubbing an Act of Parliament
over your skin

Later   the season dies
and turns bright red

Salads   the older ones
are very bitter

Boil leaves in the water
in which they cooked meat
then eat it alone

The ache – identified
from a distance by its dead-red –

should leave

*

Pineapple from Alaska:
crush a bit and you quickly learn
this epithet –

stinking

– having once been found useful

*

In older cemeteries
everyone knows
a gentleman called Mr. Rich

I hardly escaped with my life

Take our horses   They are
most vulnerable at this time

*

Heart-shaped graveyard
spreads
far from where it was

If a colony springs up
seeds will not be produced

*

Wild Europe
Canada – the 13th century general
mentioned other places valuable
as a thickener to soups: India
Persia
Massachusetts
New Jersey

Prostrate among the corn there
creeping on the ground
must give reason to wonder
if you really want it

*

Creeping Jenny reproduces
along ditches

Creeping Charlie can heal
human wounds
as well as those of snakes

*

Hawk in fields:
formidable

Bristly
hairy runners
may be found

*

Like lion's teeth
each is composed of many

Pull it apart
Study each carefully
You will see
each is entire!

Easily detached Irish children
for countless generations
wet the bed

*

Foalfoot
dove dock

moist clay soil

along stream banks
brooks
or dripping water

In seventeenth century translation
they take in the fume of dried leaves
for which bees must indeed be grateful

*

The evening sends up fever
Rocky Mountains
closed during the day

Fragrance becomes apparent

As the sun rises
blossoms droop

Their summits are very long-lived

*

Long before the nineteenth century   Hugo
made his theory of parsnips

convinced that eating the root increased
one's capacity for wine

I have not found this to be so

The old dead are not
in need of healing

*

To make whole in the sixteenth century
came from beyond the sea

Goldenrod is very sad   They have
no just reason for hating

the people of Alabama
this lovely state   its undeserved
evil reputation

*

Seaside will never bother you
unless you own some shoreline

Even then this will not disturb you
where high tide makes a line

Even the experts are salt-loving

*

Velvet during the first year
candle wicks become
smaller

All of them densely hairy
give a good grip as she lands

Each of two chambers contains
pastures

*

There are few with so many names
The Roman name means Julius

Caesar defeated American Indians   Roman ladies
dyed their hair yellow   Quaker ladies
rubbed young leaves against their forbidden
cheeks

Awful when I tried it!

*

Night-flying moths
coated with purple hairs
appearing at one time

opening many-seeded capsules
south to the Gulf

*

The moth has attracted far less attention
than its failure
to have more than one name

Looks like a moth?
There is not a shred of evidence

Were all to open at once
the moth should give you no further trouble

*

Who has not marvelled at
a presidential campaign? The American Indians

were crushed   uprooting
this very American plant
rough to the touch

*

Nothing can be compared
to Barbara caught in thunderstorms:
smooth
shiny
sweetly-scented
favoured

Introduced a second time
already here

*

Thinking as a weed may seem
strange not charming: juice
blisters the intestines of cattle
and your skin

The cup seems to glisten in sunlight

*

Beggar become human:

simple
toothed
a bit further down
covered with barbs

*

A stroll through an
unattended garden:

it may take a long time

to remove your clothes

carried far
before being dropped

Sometimes the flowers
are missing

*

Bitter buttons bring
abortions

After death   the plant
was of help

placed within winding sheets
to inhibit worms

This early escape
from colonial flowering
is deep
narrow
toothed

*

Five-finger John
does not have five
but three

touching the earth
a remedy
for impoverished soil
you may not see again

*

It is difficult to dislike
Susan   Linnaeus' great teacher

No doubt
a stowaway on trains coming east

*

The faintest disturbance and they explode
making inaudible noise
almost

May be difficult to observe
in the deep shade
of the stream banks where it lives

An antidote to poison

*

Effects a connection with the host
by stealing water
food

Will attach itself to just about any
gold thread

*

Whole lawns are composed
of stonegrass

Indeed   growing pure
might be one solution:

bright blue-green
growing happily
between the streets of large cities

solitarily
or in groups of two or three

*

Star
wherever stems touch the ground
seeds a mild winter:

a most successful shape

*

Don't be fooled by the size
In two hundred years
a one-chambered star
will probably vanish
from America!

*

In various turnings
flocks of virgins
disclosing their beauties
staining their lips with fruit

Makes a delightful picture
doesn't it?

*

The soul

at the approach of storms
bends downward

*

A four leaf clover is not four leaves

Leaflets fold at the storm   This helps
account for bumblebees

Each flower turns white

Clover will soon fill
all the spaces of bluegrass

*

Solitary flowers in the field
falsely suggest
more are present:

snake cuckoo
thunder flower
bull rattle
white robin

*

Rattle your intentions:
there is a distinct danger

that should you pick
white flowers
you will be hit by lightning

*

Night is not armed
The closely-related horse
is called Wonderberry

If you pull
any horse on your property
wear thick gloves
and beware the armament

*

Blind dogs do not
go out of their way   Most
avoid eating
because it is distasteful   Juice
will appear at the break
The Swedes got thirty ropes
for one piece of bread

*

They can be separated
by a touch –
thus

Carried far and wide by the wind
have a stimulating
effect on the heart

*

Asking fateful questions
becomes a pasture   the golden centre

a complete flower   Be sure
to get underground

*

North Carolina is well-known
and well-liked

but false   If you study
you see a waviness
in the golden eye:

poorland flower
poverty weed
moon penny
dog blow

*

Pigs have been poisoned
Man can also be poisoned
and when bruised
emit a somewhat unpleasant
variety of illnesses

*

Red ink used in cooking
should be changed at least twice
and thrown away

A fugitive with
poisonous principles
thought of putting a leaf on his foot

got his foot well soon after
cut off above ground level

*

Rebellion
under happy conditions

Within the forking branches
the solitary trumpet
reaching halfway

Poisonous mad apple

Angel's?
Devil's?

*

Doctrine assumes that a human
broken
passing through the area
would rejoin   It was obvious
to our ancestors

Occasionally one does find
small perfect blue flowers

*

Poor man's tongue
known for its pepper

Heart rolls with the wind

*

Wallflower
because of small pointed ears

Single

Common

Waste all year
elsewhere

*

Never found for three hundred years:
little boxes

pastoral maidens once carried

*

Bamboo knot
difficult to root out
adds to the perennial
ugliness in a garden

May be neglected
as the showy fruit
forms papery tissue

Enclose it

*

Lace collars
delicate
lovely

like a bird's nest
black in its deep purpleness
smelling orange

*

Commerce – it has been suggested –
will improve the disposition

No evidence has been recorded in America

*

Achilles said at Troy
one will dream of
one's future beloved

divided into a thousand parts
legs bruised
if you try to fight

*

Sweet to visit earlier

to shoot animals to eat

inducing internal bleeding
more fragrant than wrinkled

*

It was along railroad tracks as a youth
I first saw colonial maidens
gathered
broken
but given a special luster

Close inspection reveals
venereal disease

I had not the slightest idea what it was

and worse   I did not care!

Hot brine is said to help

*

Sorrel
slightly bent
never gets larger

When bitten
sourness arises
in soup

Female
tipped with three bright
feathery stigmas
hence the name

The roadside takes on a red glow
in the eighteenth century

*

The point of wings:
bumblebees

Each blossom makes horses
tremble against
the coming of a tempest

*

The lovely blue funnel-form
makes it difficult to think

It spreads so fast
we are entirely drunken

*

Arrived from Europe
we are not wanted

I have yet to encounter
even one human being

*

It has forty-six chromosomes
the human being

We too seem to take over areas
where we are not wanted
Solitary blue flowers
are far far rarer

*

Blue devil blossoms are not fragrant
to us

but the bumblebees visiting them
are very long lived

*

Devil has not been
confirmed by modern science

known by so many names
seems happiest
under these conditions

May dominate the landscape
stand out against the bright blue

Is so disliked
the government has strong poison

*

Ragged sailors make a fine
salad

Only one blooms at a time –
a very short time
opening early
closing by noon
not exactly
the real withering

*

Almost every state in the Union
has outlawed it   A blessing

if sex has sprung up in your garden

*

Creeping is very difficult   The
generally reserved English Minister
fails
upset about this

God keep us!

The British point this way and that
to fight impossibly   Canada is

dangerously armed

The head flies away
unattached to anything

*

Runaway to northern Canada –
a strong hint this member of the family
can be stubborn

*

Cat's foot on its creeping
is given away

One white spot

Stalking can be bitter

*

Heart-of-the-earth is every
gardener in the world
Our own babies withstood
rigorous modern medicine

If you happen to be in England
you might check on John

– not entirely without charm

Members of the family may be infected
with heal-all
which actually heals nothing

*

Joe Gravel-root
as an antidote for poison
gave his name   which
would otherwise have been forgotten

A close relative
was an herbal doctor

one of the taller
who would tower above you
speckled with dark purple

No flowers are present
in the boneset
abandoned fields

*

Queen
borders moist woods
streams
ditches

King
comes with parachute attached
directly from
our own Northeast

arrives on your land
may be removed by pulling

*

The medicine contained

profound depression
laboured respiration
dilation of pupils:

all the symptoms
a man in love endures

Boiling water
removes the dangerous principle

*

Despite these frightening facts
the young make delightful asparagus
Cargoes of fine silken hair
fill their beds
on the side away from the gorgeous

Leaves will bleed milk if damaged
like saddlebags

*

School boys are often guilty

or were
in the days when life was still
simple and sweet

*

If you know what rhubarb looks like
the resemblance is superficial

Robust
deeply buried

you may have –
unknowingly
– other strengths

*

During one of your nature walks
break
into rose-purple

before gradually assuming
a darker hue

*

A walk in the woods in late September
can leave you nearly smooth

*

Readers may question someone
who has done what I have done:

pulled off the road
just to stop and stare

Flaming beauty chokes out
with its feet in water

Sometimes stunning colour
is derived from blood

*

It is not wanted:
a papal tiara

sterile
fluted
hollow

may unknowingly be interpreted
as a horse's tail

will remain alive until autumn
destroying principles

*

Horses are particularly susceptible
to poisoning by this administration

It has already reached the last stages:
maidens in the seventeenth century
lacking Brillo pads

*

Few can tolerate sunlight

What appear to be individuals
are produced along the margins

Unwound croziers make
serious plants without flowers

*

Most troublesome cascades fall
into colonies of the government

*

Ada reports that
the moors and mountains of Scotland
are barely seen

Grayish and wooly
Resistant

Seems to offer some hope

*

Mirror images of each other:
dragon
orchid

*

So perfect that
every major civilization
is based on grass!

*

Brightly coloured
usually subterranean

Giant fruit of the evening
source of all life
meant to keep you

*

Carried by wind
through the mirror   images
giving rise to an entirely
new system:

thorn   prickle
and spine

*

Aliens in human affairs
get their names
in New York
*

Looking down from above
the ultimate flower:
not the rose

the potato

*

ACKNOWLEDGEMENTS

These pieces derive from two books that aimed to educate their readers about success in human culture and in the natural world: *Health, Safety and Success*, an undated school textbook "authorized for use in Manitoba and Saskatchewan," published in the late 1940s or early '50s, and *Wildly Successful Plants*, published in 1977 (adapted and reissued in 2003 as *A Field Guide to Weeds*). The rendering of prose texts on success into poetry, arguably the least commercially successful literary form, will, I hope, appeal to those with a sense of irony. But they should also be mindful that poetry, like the weed, continues to win a spiritual victory by being so difficult to eradicate entirely.

Normal Saskatchewan: Adapted from *Health, Safety and Success*, by J. Mace Andress, I. H. Goldberger, Grace T. Hallock & Elizabeth Smith, Instructor in Health, Provincial Normal School, Regina (Ginn & Company, undated, circa 1950)

Wildly Successful: Adapted from *Wildly Successful Plants*, by Lawrence J. Crockett (Collier Books, 1977), and *A Field Guide to Weeds* (Sterling Publishing, 2003)

Thanks to the Ontario Arts Council and its grant recommenders for financial assistance, to Dale for the cover photo, and to Dale and Emma for source materials.

Glen Downie worked in cancer care in Vancouver for many years, and now lives in Toronto (and at www.glendownie.com). He served a term as Writer-in-Residence at Dalhousie University's Medical Humanities Program, and won the Toronto Book Award for his 2007 *Loyalty Management*. He has letterpress-printed signed broadsides by Canadian and American poets (available through www.talltreepress.com). His most recent collection is *Democratic Beauties*, published by Tightrope Books.